RAILWAYS NORTH OF NOTTINGHAM IN THE LATTER DAYS OF STEAM

Part Two: *BULWELL to KIRKBY, MANSFIELD and WESTHOUSES*

Malcolm Castledine

BOOK LAW PUBLICATIONS

"Dedicated to my wife Dorothy
and son Mark whose perseverance,
tolerance and patience did
not go unnoticed."

First published in the United Kingdom by Book Law Publications 2004
382 Carlton Hill, Nottingham, NG 4 1JA
Printed & bound by
The Amadeus Press
Cleckheaton, West Yorkshire

INTRODUCTION

Having signed my life away over a sixpenny stamp as an indemnity to British Railways, I now possessed a trackside photographic permit which allowed me access to the indicated sections of the following lines: Ruddington to Kirkby Bentinck on the Great Central; Daybrook to Kimberley on the Great Northern; and Radford to Kirkby on the old Midland Leen Valley route. Now I could roam far and wide over an area which was fairly big.

There were no high visibility vests in those days, the authorities expected you to rely on your eyes, ears and common sense.

During my travels up and down the tracks I met many of the staff, particularly signalmen to whom I reported to with my permit. Trackside staff, platelayers, gangers, surveyors all got to know me and were generally a helpful bunch. Of course many of them probably wondered what my state of mind was but nevertheless respect was always shown, well nearly always. One day whilst tramping through snow between New Basford and Bulwell, I met one ganger who remarked "You must be b. . . . . barmy". He was probably right as the temperature was way below freezing. However, I got some smashing pictures, but I think I came back by bus.

On one occasion, wandering by Annesley South signal box, the Bobby shouted down to me "Got a minute mate?" I wondered what he wanted because usually, after reporting to one signalman who would then pass word down the line, nobody else would bother me. Anyway I got my photo permit ready to show him as I climbed the steps into the box. When I walked through the open doorway he said "Pull two numbers out of this bag and tell my mate on the other end of this phone". There are not many railway photographers who have drawn the Annesley Tote.

Tramping the lineside many engine crews got to know me and they would leave notes or word at New Basford shunters room such as "Has Blondie (as I was known to them) got a picture of us on so and so last week?" I always responded where I could and it paid dividends. One particular fireman, Chris Ward, who I'd photographed, spent years tracking me down after I had published an article on Bagthorpe Junction. He knew then that I was still about and went through the phone book, found me and we were reunited. Since then he has been a great help with memories and being able to identify things, jogging my flagging memory - after all were talking about incidents which took place forty years ago.

When I was a mechanical engineer at Wilford power station (steam was also my living as well as a hobby), many ex railwaymen got jobs as stokers and I was often stopped by men I didn't recognise "I know you" they would say "You used to wander up and down the GC main line with your cameras didn't you. I was a driver/fireman at Colwick/Annesley". Most railway staff were genuinely interested in what I was doing. The Bagthorpe Bobby once held a Western Region 'Hall' for me to photograph; once they had spotted me and my cameras even the engine crew understood in the end why they had been 'held'.

During winter, activities could be somewhat restricted so I took up night photography - what a frustrating learning curve that was. Many negatives went in the bin but those that worked made it all very satisfying and worth the time, effort and cost.

All too soon it was all over, steam had gone, stations, lines and routes were left derelict and decaying. Eventually it was swept away and new development took over. Where I once lived by Bagthorpe it is impossible to see where the railway had once been - luckily I have lots on film.

If I had a favourite on the GC then (all of them were good) perhaps a 'Green Arrow' or, as an old Annesley driver once said to me "a Black Sparrow" no doubt from the days when they were painted in British Railways lined black mixed traffic livery. However, the V2's used to get my attention at night when, from my bedroom, I could hear them working up the grade of the GC main line all the way from starting out at Victoria to Bulwell viaduct where they would ease off and quiet would once again descend. Wonderful memories indeed.

Nowadays, I spend much of my time printing those photographs from thirty to forty years ago and, 'to keep my hand in' so to speak, I also perform driving and firing duties at the Rutland Railway Museum at Cottesmore. So, steam is still coursing through my veins after all those years.

Malcolm Castledine
Nottingham, 2004.

2

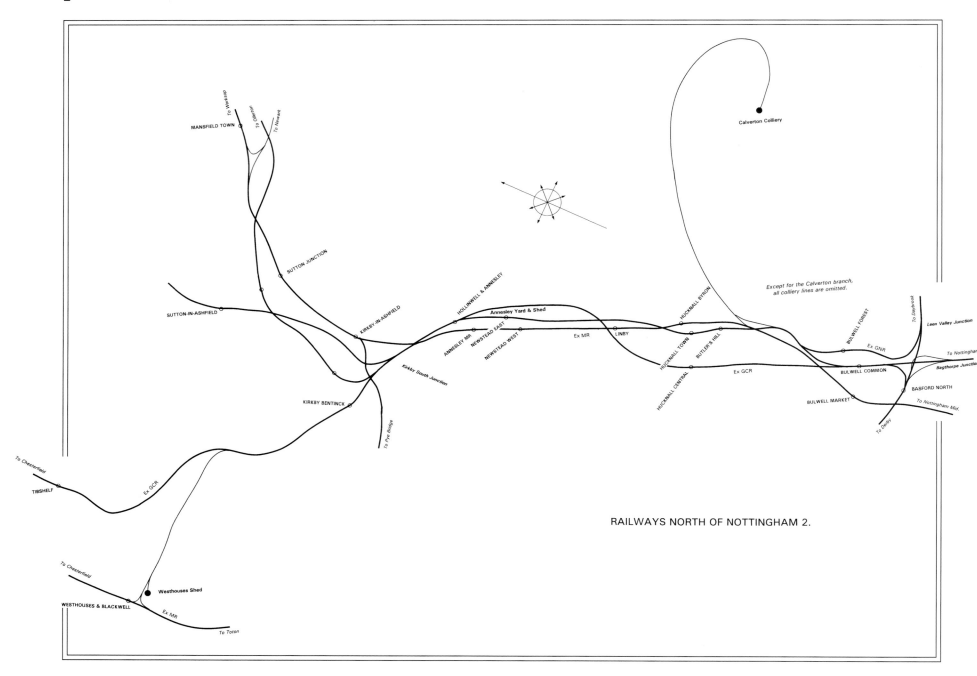

RAILWAYS NORTH OF NOTTINGHAM 2.

Bulwell Market was the Midland station serving the district of Bulwell and it was situated in a prime spot nearby to local shopping. The bridge in picture carried Highbury Road over the railway and appears to be the original structure from the 1840s where a mixture of cast iron, stone and brick was used in the construction. Another Kirkby-in-Ashfield 4MT tank engine, 42232 starts away from Bulwell Market with a Nottingham-Mansfield service on 21st March 1964 - next stop Hucknall. This engine left the East Midlands in October 1964 ending up at Tebay on the West Coast main line pushing trains up Shap.

Continuing our little jaunt along the Midland's Leen Valley line, we stay at Bulwell Market and observe an 8F rounding the curve with a train of loaded coal hoppers on 21st September 1963, probably bound for Staythorpe power station. No.48143 was a Kirkby-in-Ashfield engine at this time, having arrived from Toton shed in March 1962. In May 1964 it went to Nottingham Midland shed and then on to Westhouses in April 1965. From there it went to Colwick in October 1966 and was condemned a month later. Its last journey was to Hull where it was cut up in Drapers scrapyard. Note the trolleybus wires spanning the bridge for services No.43 and 44.

Over now to Bagthorpe Junction and the GC main line. Coming off the line from Basford North, 8F No.48382 has a train of iron ore empties as it joins the GC main. This train has just come up the gradient from the 'Rat hole' which burrowed under the former GN Derbyshire & Staffordshire main line and the GC via a short tunnel and a 90 yard long tunnel. This is the point where the GC and GN parted ways in the Down direction and joined forces in the Up direction.

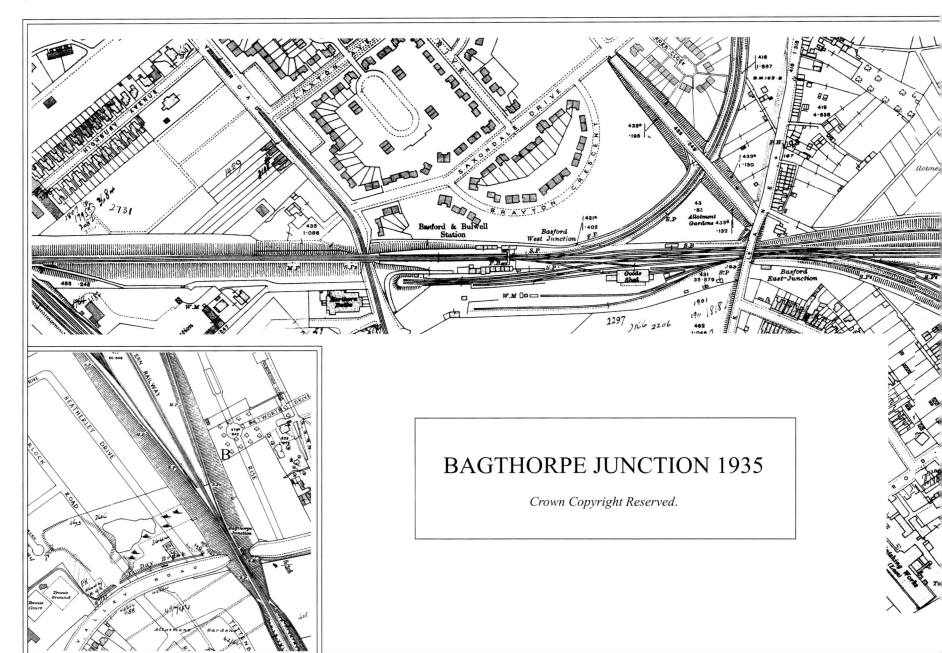

BAGTHORPE JUNCTION 1935

Crown Copyright Reserved.

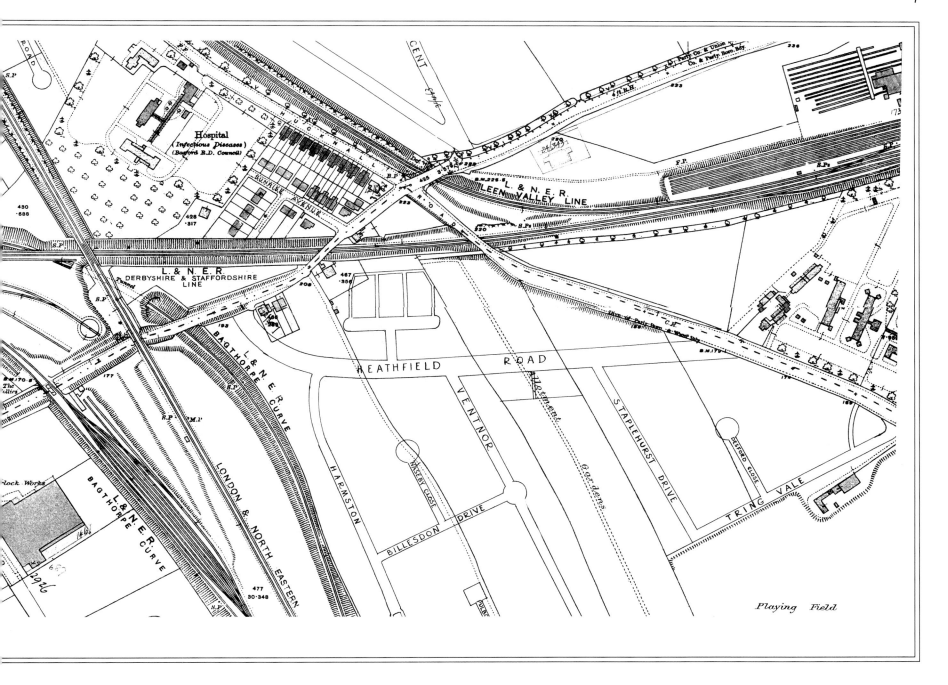

Coming up out of the 'Rat hole' line at Bagthorpe Junction, on 13th November 1965, is WD 90606 and 9F 92144, both of Colwick shed. Again Bagthorpe box has put the 'light' WD on the front of the 9F hauled empty coal train to reduce line occuation through the tunnels to Victoria. The 9F was a recent arrival to Colwick and was thrown into all sorts of traffic during its short two month stay at the shed. Having arrived with ten more 9F's in October 1965, seven of the eleven, including 92144 had been condemned by Christmas.

(opposite) When the turntable at Annesley shed was out of action, engines used to travel down to Bagthorpe Junction turn on the triangle at Bagthorpe, Basford North and Bulwell. So as not to take up too much line occupation, the engines often travelled in pairs or as in this case in three's. On the evening of 15th June 1963 B16/3 No.61434 of York, a visiting WD and one of Annesley's 9F's, start the switch which will turn then around from the way they are facing here. The 9F will want to face south, the B16 north and the WD likewise.

Before taking part in the mass cull of BR steam locomotives during the 1960's, William Rigley's at Bulwell Forest built, repaired and scrapped wagons. Being, as it were, virtually on the doorstep of a large and busy coalfield with numerous potential customers nearby, the company was engaged in all types of wagon renewal and repair and had fully equipped workshops for the purpose. However, with the decline in freight traffic, including coal, on BR during the early 1960's, the company had one last bash before closure and this time taking on the scrapping of many types of steam locomotives from various classes. Amongst those known to have been cut up at Bulwell Forest are: ex LNER types: B1 - 61126, 61334; K1 - 62013, 62032, 62038; O2 - 63925, 63926, 63927, 63928, 63932, 63935, 63936, 63937, 63938, 63939, 63941, 63945, 63956, 63962, 63964, 63972, 63973, 63974, 63977, 63980, 63985, 63986, 63987, 63989; O4 - 63914: ex LMS types: 'Crab' - 42792; 'Patriot' - 45535.

(opposite) **Three O2's, with No.63927 nearest the camera, wait in a refuge siding at Leen Valley junction for acceptance into William Rigley's scrap yard at Bulwell Forest on 11th April 1964. No.63927 had been condemned at Retford shed in the previous September and was one of the twenty-four O2's purchased for scrap by William Rigley's during 1963. This engine was no stranger to these parts as it had spent two periods at Colwick shed during WW2. Note that the cast smokebox number plate is still attached to the locomotive. This view, looking towards Daybrook, shows some of the more interesting signals which controlled the junction. Just to the right of 63927 is the site where the Workhouse siding branched off to the right.**

Some months later, rebuilt Patriot No.45535, formerly named SIR HERBERT WALKER K.C.B., but now without any nameplates, stands separated from its tender in Rigley's yard at Bulwell Forest, on Saturday 12th September 1964. The engine was withdrawn from service at Carlisle Kingmoor shed some eleven months previously but had taken this long to find a buyer and then be transported to that buyer's yard. Of course during this particular period of railway history there were more condemned steam locomotives waiting for scrapping than at any other previous time in railway history. By now private scrap yards were getting rid of the bulk of the engines whilst the British Railways workshops were doing less cutting up for various reasons. Rigley's yard remained operational, cutting up steam locomotives and old rolling stock until early 1966. It was physically connected to the BR lines until Sunday 6th March 1966 when the former Great Northern signal box at Bulwell Forest was closed and the rail connection severed.

12

Going back to Leen Valley Junction on Saturday 11th April 1964, we have some live steam in the shape of Stanier 8F No.48304 with a 16B Annesley shed plate. The 8F had been at 16B since its arrival from Cricklewood in September 1962 and would leave Annesley in June 65 for Kirkby-in-Ashfield. The 8F is waiting by the signal box after performing the daily shunt of any wagons in the yard, and Wrigley's wagon works on the GN line. This daily shunting duty also covered the tripping of condemned engines as required from storage here to Wrigley's. 48304 would return to shed via Basford North, the tightly curved spur to Bulwell Common and then the GC main line to Annesley. This particular photographic opportunity was kindly arranged by Mr Robinson, the then Station Master at Basford North. He also had responsibility for New Basford station, so he knew me very well indeed.

Seen from Arnold Road overbridge, on Saturday 16th April 1966, is the track materials recovery train with one of Colwick's Stanier Black 5's No.44830 working its way slowly backwards along the abandoned Leen Valley line towards Basford North. Notice the far from ideal coal in the tender.

Just beyond Bagthorpe Junction, going north and staying on the GC main line and still climbing, we pass over Arnold Road, Basford and then, within a 100 yards or so, we pass over the Great Northern line which had taken that company into the Nottinghamshire and Derbyshire coalfield and then on into Staffordshire. Here 8F No.48166 is about to roll onto one of the GC route's few level stretches as it crosses the bridge with a heavy mineral train on 28th September 1963. Below, on the single siding which runs alongside the GN, is a set of old LMS coaches, stabled now for the winter perhaps as the seaside excursion season, barring a few Blackpool illumination trips, is virtually over.

(opposite) In order for the GNR to gain access to Victoria station without crossing the GC main line, they had to dig this single line burrowing junction from their west to east line. After a falling gradient of 1 in 99, the line levels out as it passes under the GN main line, it then emerges for a few yards before diving into a 90 yard tunnel (known officially as Basford tunnel and unofficially as 'The Rathole') which burrowed beneath the embankment supporting the GC line. From here it climbs up a 1 in 100 gradient to Bagthorpe Junction where access to the Up GC main is made. On 22nd August 1964, Ivatt Cl.4 No.43156 drifts down the curving bank towards the aforementioned hole with a 'local' from Derby (Friargate). In the background, is Basford North Junction where the Down line from Bagthorpe Junction comes in from the left. Beyond Park Lane bridge can be seen Basford North station; only a couple of weeks remain before this station and all the others on this route out to Derby are closed.

Colwick's Ivatt Class 4 Moguls were regular performers on the Nottingham (Victoria) - Derby (Friargate) stopping trains and on 11th April 1964 No.43091 climbs the bank up to Bagthorpe Junction from Basford tunnel.

(opposite) A filthy Ivatt Class 4 No.43059 blasts out of the 'Rathole' tender first with a stopping train from Derby to Nottingham on 21st December 1963. Note the frost coated sleepers which would not see the sun all day during the winter months. The tender still has the bracket for the tablet catching mechanism attached so giving away this engines former life before Colwick.

On the opposite side of the GC main, the GN's Down connection to its main line at Basford from the GC main, came off at Bagthorpe Junction nearly opposite where the Up line joined. From there the single line dropped down a gentle slope towards Basford North but on the way it passed first the former GN carriage sidings, over Arnold Road and then past an engine stabling point complete with a 54ft 9in. turntable. This view of WD 90002 on 30th May 1964 shows it passing over the Arnold Road bridge with a Stanton iron ore train, the first four wagons being company hoppers. Notice the ornate concrete boundary fence surrounding an adjacent factory situated on Barlock Road.

Seen from the north side of the junction near Park Lane, another Stanton iron ore train rounds the curve from Bagthorpe Junction to join the GN Derbyshire main line at Basford North. O4/8 No.63819 is in charge of this Ilkeston bound train on 28th September 1963. Prior to 1948 the LNER, and GN before it, had called this area Basford & Bulwell junction with the nearby station having the same title. However, BR did not want to confuse either the public, their customers or themselves with similar names bounding around the ex LMS (MR) premises in the district so, names were changed.

On the same day, as the previous view, but now looking from the south side of the junction, we have Cl.4 No.43060 approaching Basford North with a Derby service. Behind the train can be seen numerous coaches in the carriage sidings, most now having just occasional use in excursion service. This engine, one of Colwick's since 1962, was three months away from withdrawal.

All is not what it seems here. This long mixed freight seemingly approaching Basford North from the Leen Valley Junction direction and headed by Colwick WD 90383, is in fact just starting off after having been shunted 'out of the way' to allow a Derby local passenger train to pass on 15th August 1964. This working is apparently an extra and is composed of oil tanks, wagons with old sleepers, container flats and is carrying, amongst other things, a large number of military front loading tractors (**Michigans**) on Lowmac wagons. The train was making such slow progress that it was decided to set it back up the Leen Valley Junction line to allow the Derby train to overtake. Having at last got the board 'off' we see it setting off towards Basford North and the Derby direction. Five years previously this caption could have read "...coming round the back line from Colwick yard...".

9F No.92083 of Birkenhead has the Colwick-Stanlow oil empties easily in hand on the gentle gradient from Bagthorpe Junction. It is now 30th April 1966 and compared with the last but one view (from virtually the same spot) change is evident. Gone is the coaching stock and the rails which formed the yard. Only the single line from Bagthorpe junction and the siding on the right exist. Already the town planners and developers are making plans for new roads, housing and small industry - they didn't have long to wait to implement them. The GC main runs across the background and at left the Leen Valley junction line is now defunct

(opposite) **Sporting the usual coat of filth, grime and water staining, WD 90259 passes Basford North station signal box with an eastbound freight on 28th March 1964. The stone built goods shed in the background must have been the inspiration for the GC version at New Basford goods yard. Note the point rodding emanating from the base of the ninety lever frame signal box.**

An unidentified Ivatt 'mogul' running tender first and a B1 running chimney first accelerate into Basford North in August 1964 with a train for Derby from Skegness. The goods yard and the associated loop, leading under Park Lane bridge, are seen on the right, where a railway employee cycles up the platform ramp to meet the train.

(opposite) Another eastbound but this one is a parcels train with named B1 No.61003 GAZELLE of Immingham shed in charge. Its early morning on 11th April 1964 at Basford North station and in less than six months passenger services to this station will cease as will all such services on this line. Looking out towards the horizon is something the GNR did ninety years previously as they strove to push this line out to the mines around the Erewash Valley and the lucrative coal traffic.

Rounding the curve from Bulwell Common and approaching Basford North on 28th March 1964, Stanier 8f No.48142 from Annesley shed, heads westwards with a heavy coal train probably bound for the Stanton ironworks. The engine is looking typically deplorable for the period but Annesley shed was hardly bursting with cleaners during the latter years towards run down. As part of the continual trend to rid the shed of useful motive power, 48142 was sent to Toton in August 1965, then onto Colwick in January 1966 only to become involved in that particular shed's run-down to closure. In July it managed to find a home at Kirkby-in-Ashfield but in November 1966 it was withdrawn and sold for scrap to Draper's in Hull.

(opposite) **Basford North, 1st June 1965** - closed, awaiting demolition. The station is not quite derelict yet but it might as well be. Passengers will no more tread its platforms or bridge, wait in its rooms or warm themselves by its open fires during winter. The substantial stone-built main building on the Down platform included the Station Master's house and all the official railway rooms. Those chimneys are a work of art and no doubt had plenty of 'draw'. On the Up platform wood sufficed for the waiting rooms and conveniences. As if oblivious to the plight of the station, Birkenhead 9F No.92105 blasts through with the daily Colwick - Stanlow oil empties. From Monday 2nd October 1967 all traffic formerly using this route was barred, the inevitable closure had arrived.

In a bid towards variety, we feature another 'Jubilee' on these pages in the shape of 45581 BIHAR AND ORISSA, another Farnley Junction engine which was a regular performer on the GC main line (45562 ALBERTA figured prominately in Volume One). The date is 22nd August 1964, the train is the Saturdays Only Bradford-Poole, and the location is Ha'penny bridge at Bulwell Common South.

One year later on 31st August 1965, at virtually the same location, and O4/8 No.63873 rolls a loaded coal train down the main line towards Basford. Without realising it at the time, this was probably the last summer when something like a decent service would appear on the GC.

Shunting the sidings at Bulwell Common from Bulwell South Junction, 8F No.48342, a recent arrival at Colwick but still wearing its former Kirkby-in-Ashfield 16E painted identification, wheezes wisps of steam on a cold 31st January 1966. Bulwell was at one time going to be the GC's main marshalling and sorting sidings but Annesley was chosen where land was cheaper and more plentiful.

(opposite) **On a wet Monday 24th May 1965, Annesley Black 5 No.44665 accelerates away from Bulwell Common towards a by now defunct Hucknall Central with an Engineers ballast train.**

By 5th November 1966, Bulwell Common station, which had been closed since March 1963, was looking quite dilapidated although the goods yard on the right still seems to be doing some business. Colwick 8F 48609 uses the Up loop and has charge of what appears to be an Engineer's train. The Up main line still 'looks the part' and is obviously being cared for.

Immingham Britannia's were regular visitors to and were usually rattling along the GC main line. With a good head of steam, chime whistle sounding and nameplate still intact, **70039 SIR CHRISTOPHER WREN** heads south with the New Clee to Banbury fish train in the early evening on 9th August 1963 at Bulwell North.

Seen at Bulwell Common, 45234's Driver on 11th May 1965 was Joe Barber who would retire and 'take the early money' as the redundancies were handed out at Annesley shed in the summer of 1965. He was finishing within three or four weeks of this photograph being taken. Joe's dad had also been a Driver at Annesley.

O4 No.63770 heads south at Bulwell alongside the Down line to Bestwood. Note the lack of pedestrian protection at the crossing. The O4 is heading a train of Stanton iron ore empties from the Staveley works on 8th February 1964.

(opposite) **Shortly before its move to Banbury shed, Annesley 9F 92087 takes the Down GN line at Bulwell Common North on 24th May 1965 with an empty mineral train.**

(above) **On the same day another Annesley 9F, 92013, has yet another train of mineral empties on the Down GN line at Bulwell and has just gone beneath the GC main line.**

Heading south along the GN line from Bestwood Junction, past the golf course at Bulwell Forest, O4 No.63770 has a loaded coal train on Wednesday 12th May 1965. In the background can be seen the GC viaduct spanning the former Midland line and the River Leen.

(opposite) **Shortly after passing beneath the GC line, the GN Down line negotiates a short rock cutting before joining the Up GN line near Bulwell Forest golf course. On 27th March 1966, B1 No.61302 makes lots of lovely smoke whilst heading an RCTS special round trip from Northampton to Northampton via Colwick, Langwith Junction, Killamarsh, Mexborough, Wath, Barnsley, Godley Jct, Stockport, Crewe and down the WCML - 275 miles. The B1 took the train as far as Wath yard where an EM1 electric locomotive took over. The driver was H.Hopwood and the guard was J.Kirk, both Colwick men. This was also the last steam hauled passenger train to pass through Nottingham (Victoria) before it closed.**

Heading south with a 'runner' on 12th May 1965, Annesley 9F No.92075 comes off Bulwell viaduct at the start of its journey to Woodford. From Bulwell Common to Annesley these trains used either the GC main line or the GN Leen Valley line.

The mines situated along the Leen Valley varied in age and size and during the 1960's most were still producing large amounts of coal for domestic and industrial use. During the period of our pictorial survey nearly all the pit yards had National Coal Board owned shunting locomotives of varying ages, designs, shapes and sizes. Bestwood Colliery had a number of industrial engines, both steam and diesel locomotives being available at its disposal and Hawthorn Leslie No.3606 of 1924, carrying the name VALERIE, was one of the outside cylinder 0-6-0 saddle tanks which worked the yard up to closure of the colliery in 1967. Here, on a glorious Wednesday 13th May 1964, the engine pauses between jobs in the colliery yard.

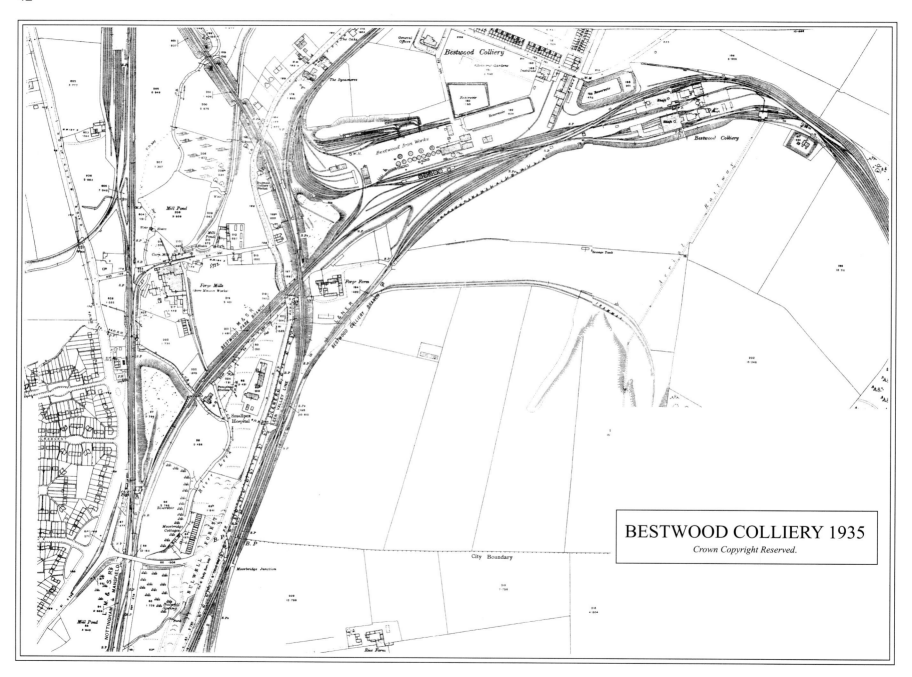

BESTWOOD COLLIERY 1935

Crown Copyright Reserved.

Collieries served by railways in the Leen Valley

ANNESLEY

Original Owners: N.H.& B. Collieries Ltd., who also owned nearby Bentinck , New Hucknall, Welbeck.

Opened: 1865.

Closed: 1994 under British Coal; re-opened 1995 by Midlands Mining Ltd. (Coal Investments), closed 1999.

Access: From Great Northern, and the Midland route.

Workforce for selective years:

	U/ground	- surface.
1946 -	676	212
1954 -	706	180
1961 -	705	178

Tonnage of saleable coal for selective years:

1946 -	288,000.
1954 -	388,000.
1961 -	455,000.
1997 -	1,500,000.

Comment: Just prior to its closure this was the oldest colliery in the country. Though having its own railway access from the GNR Leen Valley line, this curving branch largely fell into disuse from the mid 1960's and closed in 1968. The connection with the former MR line was abandoned in 1984 after about four years of disuse because in 1980 all production from the Annesley faces went out through a new drift to Bentinck for washing and loading. Two other collieries were also merged with Bentinck during the NCB period, Langton in 1967 and Brookhill in 1968. When British Coal closed Annesley in 1994 a company calling itself Midlands Mining took the place over in 1995 and started up production, which once again got to the surface via the washery at Bentinck. However, even though a new face was being developed in 1999, the colliery could not sell its coal on the British market because of cheaper foreign coal which is now being imported into the UK in ever increasing amounts.

NEWSTEAD

Original Owners: Newstead Colliery Co. Ltd., who also owned Blidworth Colliery prior to 1/1/47.

Opened: 1875.

Closed: 1987.

Access: From both Midland and Great Northern routes.

Workforce for selective years:

	U/ground	- surface
1946 -	964	313
1954 -	966	285
1961 -	1,036	214

Tonnage of saleable coal for selective years.

1946 -	500,000
1954 -	620,000
1961 -	1,054,000

Comment: Newstead Colliery village is still in situ and although basically all the properties are fully occupied, the village seems to have, like many former mining villages, an air of neglect and a feeling that something is missing.

LINBY

Original owners: Linby Colliery Co. Ltd.

Opened: 1873.

Closed: 1988.

Access: From Great Northern, and Midland route.

Workforce for selective years:

	U/ground	- surface
1946 -	745	210
1954 -	1,094	262
1961 -	906	200

Tonnage of saleable coal for selective years:

1946 -	314,000
1954 -	600,000
1961 -	1,050,000

Comment: In later years this colliery had an overhead outloading bunker erected for loading Merry-Go-Round trains.

CALVERTON

Original Owners: B.A. Collieries Ltd.

Opened: 1954.

Closed: 1999

Access: New $7^1/_2$ mile long branch line from a junction with the original Midland route at Bestwood village.

Calverton continued./
Workforce for selective years:

	U/ground	- surface
1954 -	1,068	200
1961 -	1,245	294

Tonnage of saleable coal for selective years:
1954 -   520,000
1961 - 1,041,000
1998 -   618,000

Comment: This colliery was being sunk prior to World War Two but that conflict brought the work to a halt and it was left to the newly formed National Coal Board to revive the project and eventually bring it all to fruition. MGR loading facility built. Sold by British Coal to RJB Mining in 1993. Continued to produce coal up to closure in 1999. Has large surface stocks which will take some years to clear by both train and road transport. Branch line still in use in 2004.

BESTWOOD

Original Owners: B.A.Collieries Ltd., Nottingham.

Opened: 1872.

Closed: 1967.

Access: From a branch off the Midland route just north of Bulwell station.

Workforce for selective years:

	U/ground	- surface
1946 -	1,575	500
1954 -	1,708	358
1961 -	1,672	387

Tonnage of saleable coal for selective years:
1946 -   853,000
1954 - 1,130,000
1961 - 1,081,000

Comment: The colliery washery remained open until March 1971.

RADFORD

Original Owners: Wollaton Collieries Co. Ltd., Nottingham.

Opened: Not known.

Closed: 1965.

Access: From Midland route north of Radford station.

Workforce for selective years:

	U/ground	- surface
1946 -	320	70
1954 -	463	106
1961 -	1,087	239

Tonnage of saleable coal for selective years:
1946 -   97,014
1954 - 265,000
1961 - 280,000

Comment: 1961 workforce figures boosted by merger with Wollaton Colliery which had an output of 314,000 tons in that year. Wollaton also closed in 1965.

BABBINGTON Nos.4 and 6.

Original owners: B.A. Collieries Ltd., Bestwood, Nottingham.

Opened: 1852.

Closed: 1986.

Access: Branch from a junction on the Midland route north of Basford station, and direct access from the GNR Derbyshire extension line at Babbington junction.
Workforce for selective years:

	U/ground	- surface
1946 -	600	220.
1954 -	1,567	325
1961 -	1,162	285

Tonnage of saleable coal for selective years:
1946 - 250,000.
1954 - 732,000.
1961 - 718,000.

Comment: Although this colliery did not close until February 1986, the surviving rail connection (MR) had been lifted in 1984 when all Babbington production was brought to the surface at Hucknall No.2 mine.

HUCKNALL 1 & 2

Original Owners: Sherwood Colliery Co. Ltd., Mansfield, Notts.

Opened: No.1 opened 1850's; No.2 opened 1868.

Closed: No.1 1958; No.2 1986.

Access: Both collieries had their own branches to the former Midland route. The GCR built their own branch to Hucknall No.1 mine. Hucknall No.2 mine had direct access to the Midland route

Workforce for selective years:

	U/ground	- surface
1946 -	900	290
1954 -	1,215	382
1961 -	1,038	353

Tonnage of saleable coal for selective years:
1946 - 430,000.
1954 - 750,000.
1961 - 493,000.

Comment: This colliery also had an MGR loading bunker erected and in use since early 1970's.

Calverton Colliery, situated seven miles north-east of Nottingham, did not become fully operational until 1954. The first shaft had been sunk and some of the pit head buildings erected before the conflict of WW2 halted any further progress. When the NCB came into being, they revived the works and brought the mine into production. Eventually more than 1250 men worked the colliery and by 1956 half a million tons of saleable coal was being mined; this had passed the one million tons mark five years later and that figure was usually gained each year up to its closure in 1999. Besides the sinking of the shafts and developing the working faces, this mine also needed vast earth works on the surface not least of which was a 7½ mile long double track branch line from Bestwood Junction to the colliery sidings and this was completed in October 1951. At the mine a modern wagon handling yard was laid out with fourteen arrival sidings, sixteen departure sidings and nine loading sidings at the washing plant. The complex of trackwork looked very much like a modern marshalling yard in size. To keep in line with its modern image, two 0-6-0 diesel mechanical locomotives were supplied in 1953 from Robert, Stephenson & Hawthorn one of which was named 'Calverton'. BR locomotives hauled empties onto one of two reception lines and then the NCB locomotive took over and pushed the wagons back into one of the fourteen arrival sidings. The sidings at Calverton had a capacity for 1,000 full wagons and 770 empties. This 1955 view shows the pit head on the south side of Oxton Road whilst the departure sidings are yet to feel the weight of a million tons of coal per annum. All production went to customers via the former Midland Leen Valley route.

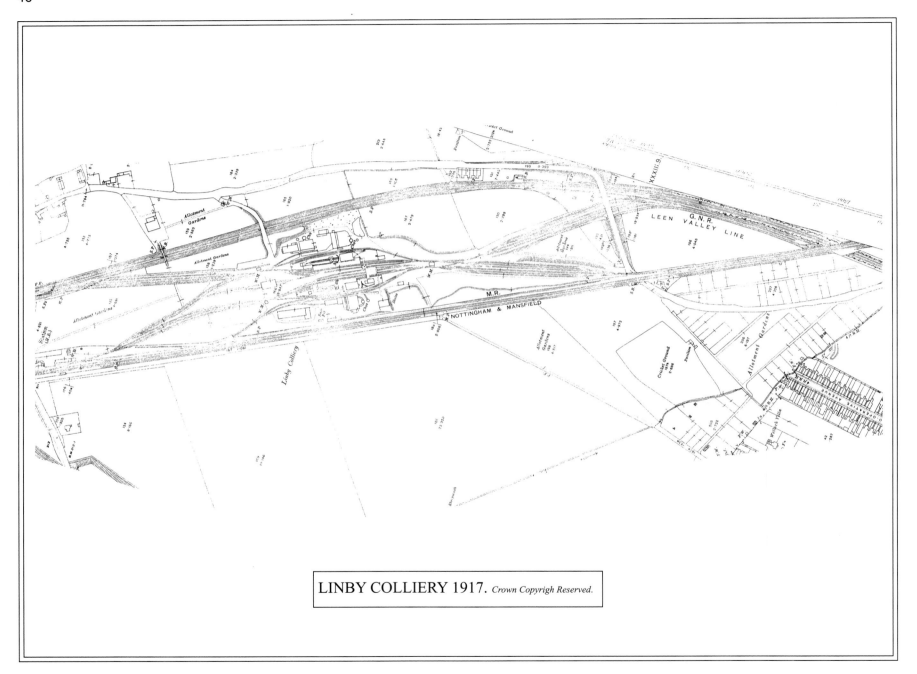

LINBY COLLIERY 1917. *Crown Copyrigh Reserved.*

Both the LMS (Midland) and LNER (Great Northern) served Linby Colliery. The Great Central, being the last railway in the area would have found access difficult on account of the elevations involved. However, the GCR had more ambitious plans so could be forgiven for neglecting this lucrative colliery. Opened in 1873, this was one of the mines which spurred on the GNR into getting its Leen Valley line built. In May 1964 this pit was producing in excess of one million tons of saleable coal a year and most of that was going out by rail; at about this time the Midland route was being favoured with most of the coal going into Toton yard. Colwick's share of the Leen Valley coal was slowly eroding, ready for closure of that yard. On 12th April 1968, Hunslet built saddle tank (2853 of 1943) named PETER, one of the National Coal Board's numerous 0-6-0s, works Linby yard.

When four Britannia Pacifics were reallocated from Neasden to Annesley shed in June 1962, to work the Nottingham - Marylebone trains, everyone was surprised. When, less than four months later four ex LMS Royal Scots were allocated to Annesley shed for the same jobs then eyebrows really were raised. The 'Scots' of course took the place of the 'Brits' which moved on to pastures new. Basically, the 'Brits' were in better condition than the 'Scots'; the LMR ruled the roost and the better locomotives were required at one of the LMR's premier sheds so they were exchanged for the run-down, clapped-out 'Scots' which would suffice at this backwater freight depot somewhere deep in the middle of the Nottinghamshire coalfield. The 4-6-0's did indeed grace Annesley's yard; in the end no less than fifteen of the class came to the shed between September 1962 and February 1964. No.46122 ROYAL ULSTER RIFLEMAN was allocated to Annesley in December 1962 from Carlisle Upperby shed and is still wearing one of that shed's 12B plates on the smokebox door in this Sunday 13th January 1963 view at Annesley. The 'Scots' did come from far and wide. If the truth be known, the call to LMR sheds from the authorities probably went something like "...bring out yer dead..." Because that is what happened regarding the 'Scots'. As each one 'gave up the ghost' at Annesley another equally as bad example would appear on the shed yard to take its place, courtesy of Crewe. Thirteen of the 4-6-0's were officially condemned at Annesley and two were 'officially reallocated' before they were condemned by Annesley, but evidence is available to show that the reallocations never did take place and the pair were withdrawn at 16B.

ANNESLEY SHED ALLOCATIONS AT SPECIFIC YEAR ENDS: 1922, 1927, 1932.

31st December 1922:

B8   4, 279, 440, 441, 446.

C14 1122, 1124, 1127, 1128, 1129.

D9 1016, 1022, 1023, 1025, 1028, 1033, 1035, 1038, 1039.

D12 428B, 442B, 443B.

12A 169B.

J10 796, 816, 835, 849, 850.

J11 227, 243, 244, 292, 294, 302, 306, 326, 327, 328, 329.

J59 421B.

L1 273, 274, 337, 343, 345, 370.

N5 764, 765, 767, 770, 774, 775, 927, 930, 937, 939.

O4 271, 351, 375, 380, 387, 389, 408, 1212, 1213, 1214, 1215, 1216, 1217, 1218, 1219, 1220, 1221, 1223, 1224, 1225, 1226, 1227, 1228, 1238.

Total 80.

31st December 1927:

B8 5004, 5279, 5280, 5444, 5446.

C12 4523.

C14 6120, 6121, 6122, 6124, 6129, 6131.

D9 6016, 6022, 6023, 6025, 6028, 6032, 6033, 6035, 6037, 6038, 6039.

D12 6464.

J10 5796, 5816.

J11 5204, 5227, 5243, 5244, 5248, 5292, 5294, 5299, 5300, 5328, 6078, 6116.

J69 7385.

L1 5340, 5343, 5345, 5366.

N5 5764, 5765, 5767, 5770, 5774, 5775, 5927, 5930, 5939.

O4 5351, 5375, 5380, 5381, 5389, 5408, 6212, 6213, 6214, 6215, 6217, 6218, 6219, 6220, 6221, 6223, 6225, 6226, 6227, 6228, 6238, 6239, 6262, 6266, 6267, 6282, 6307, 6309, 6320, 6323, 6353, 6368.

Q4 6179.

Total 85.

31st December 1932:

B7 5471.

B8 5280, 5442, 5446.

C14 6120, 6121, 6124, 6126.

D9 6016, 6023, 6028, 6032, 6033.

J10 5796, 5816.

J11 5204, 5210, 5217, 5218, 5240, 5243, 5244, 5294, 5308, 5317, 5328, 5993, 6078.

J39 2704, 2709, 2779, 2780, 2781.

K3   58, 109, 159.

N5 5051, 5748, 5758, 5764, 5765, 5767, 5770, 5774, 5775, 5930.

O4 5351, 5375, 5380, 5381, 5389, 5394, 5408, 6212, 6213, 6214, 6217, 6218, 6219, 6220, 6221, 6225, 6226, 6228, 6238, 6239, 6266, 6274, 6299, 6307, 6309, 6320, 6323, 6339, 6349, 6353, 6356, 6368, 6560, 6620.

Q4 5064, 5067, 6179.

Total 83.

On the same day that 46122 was photographed on Annesley shed yard, the storage (scrap) lines were bulging with recently condemned ex LNER locomotives amongst which was J39 No.64739, the last example of its class allocated to Annesley. This melancholy line of engines consists mainly Thompson O1's. This J39 had, since 1934, done three separate stints at Annesley, the last being from November 1957 to 31st October 1962 when it was withdrawn. The J39's were never allocated to Annesley shed in any numbers over the years, eight-coupled locomotives seemingly being the preference.

13th January 1963. Thompson O1 No.63869 had been at Annesley shed since July 1950 and almost up to condemnation on 17th November 1962, had been amongst the shed's star performers on the Woodford 'runners'. However, in September 1962 the LM Region authorities drafted in twenty-one Stanier 8F's to replace an equal number of O1's so that during the month between 26th October and 21st November 1962 all the Thompson 2-8-0's were withdrawn. To add insult to injury perhaps, this O1 was sent to Crewe works for scrapping; the other O1's went to either Crewe or Derby. J39 64739 also went to Derby for cutting-up.

Prior to the arrival of the 'Brits' in June 62, three other BR Standard locomotives arrived at Annesley earlier in the year. These locomotives were 2-6-2 tanks of the 84XXX class, Nos.84006 (April), 84007 (March) and 84027 (March). These particular tank engines came to replace the Ivatt 2-6-2Ts which had in turn replaced the Fowler 2-6-4Ts, two of them eventually left 16B and one, 84027 stayed long enough to be condemned there in May 1964. Here 84007 languishes on the eastern side of the shed yard on 13th January 1963, covered in snow and temporarily out of use. Note in the background one of the numerous sludge tenders which were ever present at Annesley's water treatment plant.

The ultimate in LMS motive power - the Stanier Pacific. 46251 CITY OF NOTTINGHAM spends Friday night, 8th May 1964 on Annesley shed prior to working an RCTS special from Nottingham (Victoria) on the Saturday morning. The Duchess represented one of the few ex LMS standard classes not to have been allocated to Annesley during the short time that the shed was under London Midland control. In January 1959 three Fowler 2-6-4T's came from Nottingham Midland shed for a one year stay before moving on to Trafford Park; these engines took on jobs such as the 'Dido'. Following right behind the tanks came five 'Crabs', two from Nottingham Midland and three from Derby; the first two stayed until November 1961 before returning to Nottingham whilst the other three all went to Burton shed during June and July 1960. Of course there were also two 'Jubilees' not to mention the horde of Black 5's which hung around till the end. However, the earliest known allocation of a former LMS engines was 8F 48678 which came to Annesley in July 1956 from Wellingborough and returned there in December of that year.

No matter which way you looked at a Stanier Pacific they just did look the part for the job.

(opposite) A final glimpse at 46251 in the evening sun of an English Spring - the admiration will last forever. Coming down to earth, this picture also captured, in the left background, a view of the mechanical coaling plant which was erected at Annesley during the LNER shed modernisation period of the 1930's.

On Saturday 11th September 1965, Annesley shed was certainly in the grip of closure fever. The place by now had only Stanier Black 5's and 8F's and many of them were dead awaiting attention, withdrawal or scrapping. Stanier 5 No.45292 (supposedly allocated to Tyseley but seemingly spending an awful lot of time working from Annesley) here over the ash pit road, stands amongst the piles of ash and clinker which has been allowed to build up through staff shortages. Soon this whole area was to be buried under millions of tons of colliery waste generated by Newstead, Annesley and Linby collieries over the next couple of decades - this spot will be sixty or more feet below the surface by 1985.

'Royal Scot' 4-6-0 No.46163 CIVIL SERVICE RIFLEMAN (nameplates missing), is well coaled with some good stuff by the looks of it, as it moves off shed on a quiet Sunday afternoon in January 1963. The engine will make its way down to Nottingham (Victoria), where it will take up an express or semi-fast working to the south.

On a cold January afternoon in 1963, BR Standard Class 2's Nos.84007 and 84027, their working days now over, are stored on a siding situated on the eastern side of the shed. These two engines, along with a third one, were transferred to Annesley to replace the two LMS Ivatt 2-6-2T used on the Dido. When the Dido ceased running one of these Cl.2's could often be found shunting New Basford carriage sidings.

On the same Sunday afternoon in January 1963 this forlorn line-up of withdrawn locomotives (one J39 and the rest O1's) stretched out into the snow - what a melancholy sight! The O1's had been withdrawn during the preceding year but had been used mainly on the famous Annesley-Woodford 'runners' prior to the coming of the Standard 9F's, after which a few were retained at Annesley for local workings.

The engine shed roof at Annesley was rebuilt in early BR days when the original wooden framed northlight roof was replaced by a steel and concrete affair. The MS&LR built Annesley as a six-road shed but had made provision for future expansion on the eastern side of the shed. In the end the expansion never materialised; Annesley engine shed, like the GC main line did not live up to the expectations of its planners and developers. By September 1965 the shed was starting to fill up with engines no longer required and two of those in view, 45333 and 44665 would be leaving for Kirkby-in-Ashfield shed within weeks. By the end of summer 1965 all the 8F and 9F freight engines had left for other sheds although one 8F, No.48378 which was stored awaiting repair, was condemned in August, the only Stanier 8F withdrawn at Annesley. It was now down to the Stanier Black 5's to take the shed into 1966.

Another view of 'visiting' 45292, now on the turntable and coaled up ready for work on 11th September. This particular turntable was apparently installed in the early 1950's and was one of the 70ft articulated types which had become standard appliances for replacement and new installations, although this one was electrically operated.

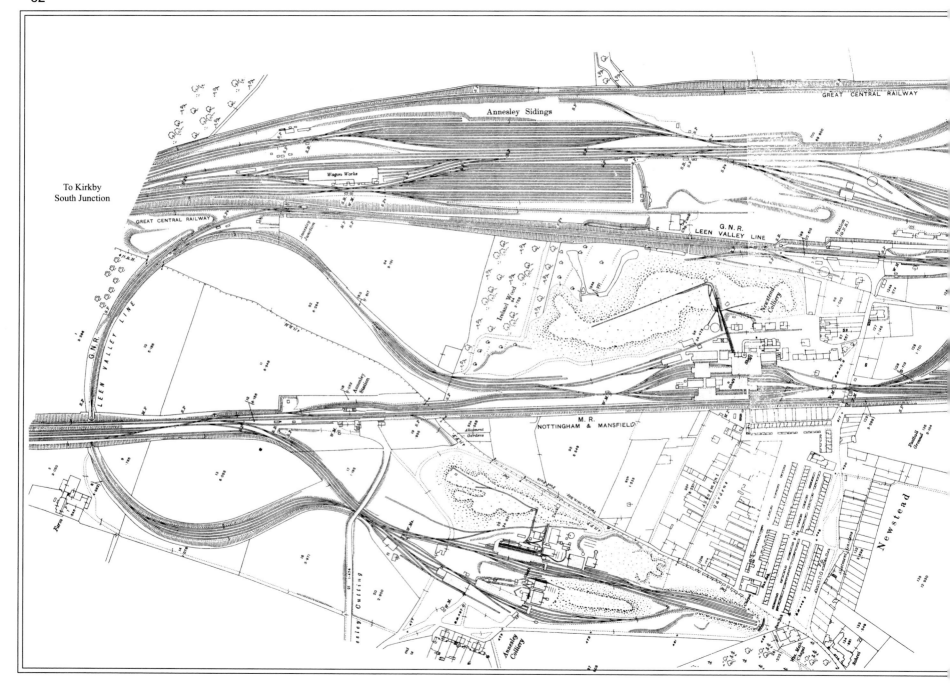

Annesley Sidings

GREAT CENTRAL RAILWAY

To Kirkby
South Junction

GREAT CENTRAL RAILWAY

Wagon Works

G. N. R.
LEEN VALLEY LINE

Station
(G.N.R.)

Newstead
Colliery

L E E N   V A L L E Y   L I N E

G. N. R.

Imhaul Wood

Annesley
Station

Allotment
Gardens

M. R.
NOTTINGHAM & MANSFIELD

Newstead

Football
Ground

Farm

Gardens

Annesley Cutting

Annesley
Colliery

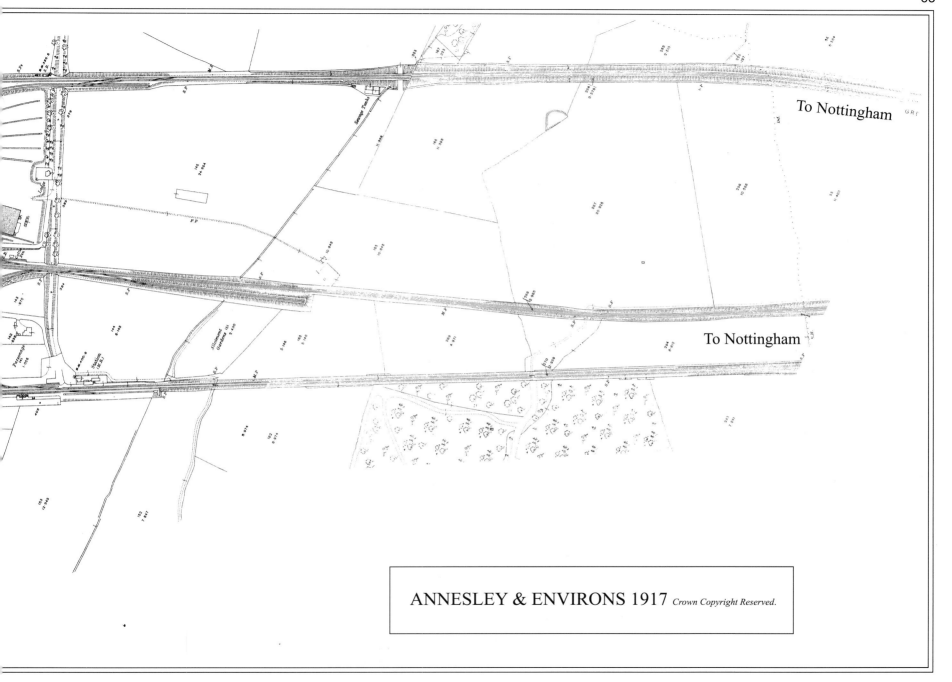

To Nottingham

To Nottingham

ANNESLEY & ENVIRONS 1917 *Crown Copyright Reserved.*

By March 1965 Annesley yard was being run down ready for closure in June. This view of Annesley 8F No.48142 shunting the Down yard on the 12th also highlights the lack of traffic in the Up yard. The three road wagon repair shop on the right was also a casualty of the yard closure but the engine shed remained operational for a while longer yet.

At least the winter sun shone on 12th March 1965. Colwick B1 No.61194 with a tender full of 'best slack' waits with a single brake van on the former GN main line alongside Annesley yard.

A line of withdrawn Stanier engines on the land bordering the east side of the shed, September 1965. Heading this bunch is 45416, condemned July. Also in the line-up are 45301 and 45335, both condemned in July. All three Black 5's and 45334, which was withdrawn in June, would end up at Cashmore's scrap yard in Great Bridge by December. The last of the four engines on this road is the withdrawn 8F, 48378 which went to a scrapyard in Newport, Monmouthshire. The last active locomotives at Annesley were all Black 5's, 44932 left in December whilst 44848 and two others departed in January 1966.

York V2 No.60828 exits Annesley yard for Woodford during the evening of 8th May 1964.

(opposite) **Stanier 8F 48141 sets out from Newstead Colliery with a loaded coal train in March 1965. This is Newstead station of Midland Railway origin which is still in use today, after being rebuilt and revived for the use of Robin Hood line passengers. The original staggered platforms no longer exist, the Up platform being done away with completely and the Down platform being moved a hundred yards to the north opposite the present Station Hotel. Note the cylindrical water tank/crane and the Home signal bracketed out over the line for better sighting.**

Kirkby South Junction, 18th April 1964. Colwick WD No.90038 comes off the GCR's Mansfield line (opened 1916) with a coal train which probably originated at Clipstone Colliery and is heading for Colwick yard. The train has now joined the GC main line and is passing over the junction with the GNR's Leen Valley Extension route to Shirebrook. The signal box here was opened in 1898, had thirty levers and was made redundant in 1968 when this stretch of railway and the junctions it controlled closed.

It wasn't intended to include a picture of FLYING SCOTSMAN in this album but this view of the engine and its special train at Kirkby South in April 1964 help to illustrate the excavation required to create these rock cuttings during the 1890's. No.4472 is coming round the curve of the GN line from Shirebrook with a Manchester to Marylebone special and has travelled over the Woodhead line passing through the new tunnel albeit with the fire run down and with an EM2 Co-Co for haulage. Thence Sheffield, Killamarsh and via the 'Clog and Knocker' through Shirebrook to Kirkby South, and is travelling rather slowly over the speed restriction on the newly laid track (note the temporary 5 m.p.h. speed restriction sign).

A parting shot of FLYING SCOTSMAN as the driver opens the regulator after the speed restriction at Kirkby South. The coal in the tender appears to be hand picked and considering the distance travelled so far by the train, there is still plenty of it.

This short coal train hauled by 63741 through Kirkby South Junction on 18th April 1964 is the reason for the concentration sidings at Annesley. When the sidings were laid down most collieries could not supply a full train load of coal each day so a pick-up or trip engine would make its way round a number of local mines collecting full loads and dropping off empty wagons before returning to the concentration sidings where the smaller consignments would be marshalled into long heavy trainloads. Why this Frodingham O4/8 is working an Annesley turn this day is unknown but the study nevertheless makes for a pleasing picture.

Just north of Kirkby South Junction the GC main line passed over the Midland's line from Pye Bridge to Kirkby-in-Ashfield and on 16th May 1964 Staveley O1 No.63589 crosses the bridge on its way to Annesley yard with a train of coal. Just above the engine can be seen the GC's Mansfield branch of 1916 curving away through a cutting to the north and east.

With a train load of empty 16-ton coal wagons, Stanier 8F No.48166 heads northwards along the ex Great Central main line in May 1964. Behind, at a slightly higher elevation, can be seen the former GCR Mansfield line which was still generating coal traffic from the Mansfield area mines. Within less than half a mile of this location there were in 1964 five separate railway routes, all of which were carrying coal traffic - a far cry from today, 2004.

The ex Great Northern Leen Valley Extension from Kirkby South Junction to Shirebrook passed over the Midland's Kirkby to Pye Bridge line just south on Kirkby-in-Ashfield. Stanier 8F No.48037 is seen drifting down hill from Kirkby to Pye Bridge just south of that location on 16th May 1964 with a loaded coal train presumably for Toton yard. This engine went to Toton shed just over twelve months later and before 1965 was out the 8F had been withdrawn and later sold to Cashmore's at Great Bridge for scrap.

At Kirkby-in-Ashfield the Midland Railway built an engine shed to serve the numerous local collieries and two of that shed's engines have charge of this heavy coal train in May 1964 en route to Toton yard. The seemingly strange motive power combination includes the old, 1927 vintage 44379 and the not so old 1954 vintage 92018. The former has but four months left in service before withdrawal whereas the latter is good for another three years but not in coal country; when the 0-6-0 went for scrap the 9F left Kirkby for greener pastures. Here the six-coupled engine has been put on the front to add that little bit of extra braking power for the loose coupled train down the gradient towards Pye Bridge; coming back to Kirkby shed the pilot engines were used as bankers or assisting engines up the steep climb. Kirkby shed, just visible behind the signal box, was taken over by diesel locomotives and they used this same route from the mines to gain the main line on the Erewash valley and then on to Toton yard. The mining of coal has virtually finished in the United Kingdom and with less than a dozen deep mines still producing in 2004 we might have seen the last of a once mighty industry. Whatever political affiliations the reader may have, there is no denying that coal mining and transportation brought a prosperity to Nottinghamshire which for 150 years shaped much of the landscape and many lives.

Westhouses shed stood just to the east of Westhouses and Blackwell station. The latter was on the main line whereas the shed was on the south side of a spur which connected a number of coal mines in the vicinity to the Midland line. The shed was built to house the locomotives serving the mines and as long as the mines stayed open, then so did the shed. However, we all now know the story of Britain's coal industry and the shed obviously went the same way. But on this the 4th day of September 1965, the shed was doing good business, albeit a Saturday, engines were arriving after their morning labours and were ready for the weekend rest. At this time the shed could boast a reasonable allocation of steam locomotives which mainly comprised Fowler 0-6-0s and Stanier 2-8-0s. For a few years before and during the war the shed housed three of the LMS Garratt's at various periods but in the main the ubiquitous 0-6-0 tender engine has been its most useful type.

(opposite) Kirkby-in-Ashfield shed had an allocation which comprised mainly of Stanier 2-8-0s but amongst the big engines there was a few vintage Midland locomotives such as this 0-6-0, one of two ancient open cab types shedded there and used for shunting at Mansfield Town goods yard. The date is 16th May 1964 and the this engine has very little time left before being scrapped.

The six road shed building at Westhouses was a typical Midland Railway straight shed construction with gabled ends, and roof bays covering two roads each. On this September Saturday the shiny new diesels are already taking up shed space, pushing outside the long time and worn-out residents. Although the steam locomotives were actually allocated to this depot, the diesels were not as they were Toton based and were stabled at Westhouses. Long after the shed closed to steam in 1966, the building housed diesel locomotives and at weekends as many as thirty could be found here. 4F No.44113 was one of the shed's last 0-6-0s, being withdrawn in January 1966. This engine was used on a local railtour on 17th October 1965, no doubt the last occasion it hauled passenger stock.

A classic study of a Stanier 8F on shed. Mirfield's No.48357 has worked in from Yorkshire on 4th September 1965 and is about to spend the weekend at Westhouses. This Horwich built engine was a wartime build being allocated new to Normanton, eventually to spend all of its life working from West Riding sheds. Having spent some time at Wakefield shed in the mid-1950s, it moved there again in February 1966 before being withdrawn in September of that year, a year after this pose. Note all the depot paraphernalia surrounding the engine - water crane, water column, tap and hose, wheelbarrows, shovel, empty brazier, coal wagons, withdrawn locomotives. There has even been an effort to clear the firebox and smokebox dregs from the concrete hard standing, even the pit looks fairly empty - not an easy task in these the latter days of steam on BR. Note the 'Peak' in the background attached to the depot breakdown van, obviously the Shed Master has seen the advantage of not having to keep an engine in steam over the weekend when all the driver has to do is 'turn the key' to fire up the diesel engine.

Another Westhouses 4F was 44243, seen attached to an 8F on 4th September 1965 and just days away from withdrawal. By December it was in the hands of scrap merchant T.W.Ward of Killamarsh and the rest is !

Indulging somewhat on 44243 perhaps, it is worth looking at the tender attached to the engine. This was one of the tenders fitted with a sliding roof over the coal space, for working on snow-plough duties. Today the sliding roof is detached, which was perhaps a fair weather procedure but one thing is certain, it would never be fitted on the tender again. The yellow painted stripe on the cabside of the 4F denotes that that particular engine was banned from working on the electrified lines south of Crewe, a ban which included hundreds of LMS engines and virtually all the classes. This angle of the exposure also allows us to view the Westhouses coaling stage which was one of the manual type employing a number of men whose sole task was to empty coal from wagons into the locomotive tenders.

Amongst the 'stored' engines at Westhouses in September 1965 were a number of the shed's 4F's, 44203 and 44278 being back-to-back and both wearing the cab stripes and electrification warning flashes. No.44203, previously of Bedford shed, was not actually condemned until seven months later in March 1966 and during the following summer it was moved to Wath for scrapping by Station Steel. Note the rubbish strewn about - two lamps and a bucket.

44278 had been on Toton's 'books' before being transferred to Westhouses shed and was one of a number 'cleared out' to make way during the demolition of the steam roundhouses and the building of the new purpose built diesel depot. This 4F is attached to another tender offering crew protection during inclement weather or when snow clearing operations were necessary. Just in front of the engine is a raised mound of earth representing the space which was to be occupied by a fuel oil tank if the abortive 'Fuel Oil Scheme' had gone ahead in 1946. The control building for the pumping and heating of the oil can be seen in the background of the first photograph featuring 44243 on page 82. No.44278 was withdrawn in January 1966 and journeyed south to Kettering for cutting up.

Tucked away further up the shed yard on 4th September 1965 was recently withdrawn WD No.90580. This engine had been Doncaster based when it was condemned in August and must have had some kind of mechanical problem to have been withdrawn here at Westhouses.

(opposite) The local passenger service between Nottingham (Midland) and Worksop ran via Mansfield (Town) and the shed at this latter place was responsible for many of the workings. At the end of the LMS era redundant but still serviceable 4-4-2Ts from the London, Tilbury & Southend line were being used, then in the early BR period Stanier 2-6-2Ts took over. Mansfield shed was closed in 1960 with the engines and men transferring to Kirkby-in-Ashfield. The 2-6-2 tanks now gave way to 2-6-4 tanks which came from far and wide looking for work after being made redundant by the ever growing tide of diesel or electric multiple units. Saturday 21st March 1964 was one of those foggy days which we took so much to be part and parcel of everyday life but which would become virtually nonexistent once the Clean Air Act came in. However, with so many steam locomotives about and nearly every household and factory burning coal, it was to be a number of years before the planned smoke free zones began to emerge. Here at Mansfield (Town) a Nottingham bound train has just arrived in platform 1 from Worksop behind Kirkby allocated exLMS 4P No.42218, itself an exile from the LT&SR line.

Appendix.

The complete LNER locomotive allocation for Annesley motive power depot from 1st January 1923 to closure.
Incorporating LMS - LM(R), and BR Standard and diesel allocations.

Note: Although these allocations 'officially' start at 1/1/23, it will be noted that where former Great Central locomotives are concerned, an earlier date is sometimes applicable and these have been duly noted.

By 11th September 1965 the Derby lot were well encamped at Annesley shed but it did not matter the place had only months of operational life left. 45190 and its cohorts would soon be gone - in more ways than one.

A5

5165/69800 18/3/11-5/1/24;
8/6/58-15/6/58.
5170/69805 10/6/11-5/1/24.
5448/69808 12/9/11-5/1/24.
5449/69809 19/10/12-22/4/24;
7/10/56-14/12/58.
5450/69810 2/11/12-5/1/24.
5128/69813 21/12/12-7/7/24.
5129/69814 28/12/12-25/3/24.
5374/69818 21/10/56-16/12/58c.
5046/69825 14/10/56-14/12/58.

B1 (B18)

5195/ 1479 21/9/47-31/12/47c.
5196/ 1480 21/9/47-31/12/47c.

B1 (Thompson)

61063 19/6/49-21/10/56.
61066 19/6/49-7/10/56.
61209 21/3/48-14/10/56.
61272 17/2/57-26/1/58.

B7

5036/ 1363 10/6/25-4/3/26.
5037/ 1364 19/7/24-22/11/24;
3/5/43-30/10/43.
5458/ 1366 24/5/43-21/6/43;
5/7/43-30/10/43.
5460/ 1368 5/9/43-30/10/43.
5462/ E1370 3/5/43-24/10/43.
5463/ 1371 19/7/24-15/11/24.
5464/ 1372 5/9/43-30/10/43.
5467/61704 24/5/43-21/6/43;
5/7/43-30/10/43.
5469/61705 31/10/35-30/10/43.
5470/ 1378 5/1/38-6/11/43.
5471/ 1379 10/2/32-by 1/1/35;
3/5/43-13/11/43.
5472/ 1380 21/7/33-30/10/43.
5031/ 1383 3/5/43-30/10/43.
5032/ 1384 19/7/24-15/11/24;
3/2/34-30/10/43.
5033/ 1385 19/7/24-8/6/25;
3/5/43-30/10/43.

5034/ 1386 24/5/43-21/6/43;
5/7/43-24/10/43.
5035/61709 10/6/25-17/4/26;
24/5/43-21/6/43;
5/7/43-30/10/43.
5476/ 1389 19/5/43-30/10/43.
5477/ 1390 24/5/43-21/6/43;
5/7/43-24/10/43.
5478/61711 24/5/43-21/6/43;
5/7/43-30/10/43.
5479/61712 24/5/43-30/10/43.
5480/ 1393 3/5/43-24/10/43.
5481/ 1394 3/5/43-30/10/43.
5483/61713 3/5/43-24/10/43.

B8

5004/ 1349 3/2/22-1/8/25;
8/11/26-16/1/28;
15/8/43-27/4/47.
5439/ 1350 10/8/43-27/4/47.
5440/ 1351 17/2/22-19/7/24;
14/11/24-25/7/25;
4/1/33-27/4/47.
5441/ 1352 6/10/22-3/11/23;
25/6/24-9/6/25;
9/8/43-6/5/47c.
5442/ 1353 15/10/28-27/4/47.
5443/ 1354 24/1/25-27/3/26;
9/8/43-27/4/47.
5444/ 1355 12/10/27-2/4/28;
15/6/43-27/4/47.
5445/ 1356 15/8/43-27/4/47.
5446/ 1357 3/2/22-3/11/23;
by 6/6/26-5/5/47.
5279/ 1358 3/2/22-19/7/24;
6/10/24-8/6/25;
8/11/26-6/3/28;
9/10/33-27/4/47.
5280/ 1359 31/3/27-2/4/28;
17/11/28-25/3/47c.

B13

752 ?/2/26-20/9/26.

This single Annesley allocated example of the NER 4-6-0 classes was used on goods turns to York and down to

Woodford. Throughout the LNER period and right into BR days, other former NER 4-6-0's of classes B14, B15 and B16 became regular visitors to Annesley, working either to the yard or beyond to Woodford.

C4

5194/ 2901 8/7/38-21/9/47.
6088/ 2912 31/10/35-8/12/46.
5360/ 2922 6/1/39-12/2/39.
5362/ 2924 23/10/35-21/9/47.

C12

4505/67363 20/2/49-31/5/53;
23/8/53-14/10/56.
4513/ 7370 28/1/40-28/7/43.
4519/67374 14/3/28-22/10/28.
4523/ 7377 ?/7/27-14/3/28.
4524/ 7378 15/2/27-?/7/27.
4537/67387 13/11/49-23/12/51.
4548/67398 22/3/30-25/4/30.

C13

6058/67403 16/5/39-28/1/40.
6063/67408 25/1/53-19/4/53.
6065/67410 16/5/39-28/1/40;
4/9/40-30/7/42.

C14

6120/67440 12/12/25-1/11/34.
6121/67441 ?/12/27-9/2/37.
6122/67442 ?/5/18-2/4/28.
6123/67443 16/5/19-24/10/23.
6124/67444 26/5/19-2/4/28;
26/1/29-16/5/39.
6126/67446 11/12/30-28/6/35.
6127/67447 23/9/21-28/12/23.
6128/67448 ?/6/18-by 9/33.
6129/67449 ?/6/18-16/1/28.
6130/67450 14/8/35-9/4/38.
6131/67451 16/2/23-2/4/28;
19/8/35-15/5/39.

D9

6016/62303 8/11/19-31/1/37.
6022 8/12/22-2/4/28.
6023/62308 4/3/21-2/11/35.
6025/ (2310) 14/5/20-2/4/28;
5/5/33-12/10/33.
6028 at 4/22-2/4/28;
29/10/28-21/6/37.
6032/ (2316) 7/4/26-12/5/39.
6033/62317 at 4/22-29/10/35.
6035/62319 at 4/22-2/4/28.
6037/62321 21/5/24-2/4/28;
16/5/29-24/7/29.
6038/ 2322 14/5/20-2/4/28.
6039/ (2323) 27/10/22-2/4/28;
15/12/31-4/1/32.
5110 14/2/26-7/4/26.

D10

5429/62650 26/1/23-10/3/23.
5430/62651 16/2/23-10/3/23.
5431/62652 10/4/37-7/1/39.
5432/62653 2/3/23-10/3/23.
5437/62658 28/1/37-8/7/38.

D12

(6463) 1/1/23-26/2/25c.
6464 20/1/21-11/3/30c.
(6465) 1/1/23-19/10/25c.
6466 2/6/25-8/10/26c.
6467 1/1/23-1/3/26c.

F1

5575 27/4/40-23/8/40.
5594 20/5/40-1/6/40.

F2

5776/ 7104 9/7/42-14/1/44;
12/2/49-30/5/49c.
5777/ 7105 5/8/45-27/8/48c.
5778/67106 16/6/48-31/12/48c.
5779/67107 16/3/47-28/2/49c.
5782/ 7110 8/7/42-31/7/42;
29/11/42-23/10/47c.

Class F2 cont./
5783/ E7111 18/2/44-10/3/46.

GC12A Class

169ʙ   1/1/23-6/6/23c.

J5

3035/65494 25/12/49-21/10/51.

J6

3536/64185 12/1/25-26/6/26.
3538/64187 12/1/25-6/9/27.
3551/64200 17/9/25-14/10/27.
3552/64201 1/9/25-6/9/27.
3553/64202 12/1/25-7/9/27.
3557/64206 16/9/25-6/9/27.

J10

5796   16/5/17-10/8/35c.
5811/65147 1/11/35-4/12/35.
5816   1/1/23-10/8/35c.
5835/65160 2/10/17-26/11/27.
5849/65169 1/1/23-28/11/27.
5850/65170 1/1/23-25/7/27.

J11

5985/64292 23/5/38-7/8/55.
5987/64294 5/3/44-8/8/48.
5993/64300 27/6/29-16/9/57c.
6010/64317 7/8/55-6/11/55.
6011/64318 30/6/33-8/8/35;
            19/8/35-5/5/57.
6047/64324 13/10/40-29/6/47;
            7/8/55-27/10/57.
5205/64332 12/5/34-15/6/34.
5210/64335 27/6/29-1/11/33.
5218/64340 27/6/29-3/11/33.
5221/64342 5/3/44-30/9/44.
5224/64345 23/1/33-7/9/33.
5227/64348 19/1/17-14/1/30.
5177/64354 1/7/45-28/4/57.
5204/64357 *by* 6/6/26-24/3/39.
5208/64359 5/5/57-?/5/59.

5217/64360 15/10/29-16/4/36.
5220/64361 23/1/33-7/9/33;
            1/7/45-16/11/47;
            13/6/48-7/8/55.
5240/64364 26/2/26-4/3/26;
            17/10/29-24/12/44;
            25/2/45-29/6/47;
            7/8/55-28/7/57.
5241/64365 1/7/45-8/8/48.
5235/64366 1/11/33-17/4/36.
5239/64370 3/11/33-20/6/55c.
5242/64371 28/5/38-12/2/39.
5243/64372 2/11/18-26/5/33.
5244/64373 17/11/16-14/3/35;
            18/3/35-19/3/39.
5246/64375 1/7/45-13/6/48;
            28/7/57-1/5/60.
5248/64377 22/9/27-23/9/30.

6078/64386 13/8/27-10/11/28;
            20/4/29-13/6/48;
            7/8/55-12/5/57.
6116/64392 7/9/27-21/2/30.
5284/64399 10/7/34-18/3/35.
5287/64402 3/12/35-27/6/36.
5291/64406 21/10/51-28/4/57.
5292/64407 22/1/16-23/5/29.
5294/64409 13/11/15-8/8/48.
5299/64414 6/9/27-?/?/??.
5302/64417 1/1/23-7/2/25.
5305/64420 28/4/57-1/5/60.
5306/64421 20/9/19-16/9/25.
5308/64423 1/1/31-26/11/34.
5317/64431 20/4/29-7/8/55.
5326/64439 19/1/09-17/9/25;
            12/5/57-?/5/59.
5327/64440 24/10/08-12/1/25.
5328/64441 5/1/09-1/9/25;
            3/10/25-5/10/25;
            17/10/25-30/6/34.
5329/64442 16/1/15-12/1/25.

J39

1495/64716 30/10/43-30/3/47.
1497/64719 30/10/43-30/3/47.
1498/64720 30/10/43-30/3/47.
1287/64738 14/3/35-9/8/43.

1289/64739 15/11/34-9/8/43;
            30/10/43-30/3/47;
            3/11/57-31/10/62c.
2694/64747 2/12/33-30/3/47;
            3/11/57-28/8/59.
2697/64750 30/10/43-30/3/47.
2704/64757 3/10/30-13/3/32;
            4/4/32-30/3/47.
2709/64762 31/10/28-24/6/29;
            20/8/29-20/6/30;
            21/8/30-30/3/47.
2710/64763 10/11/28-24/6/29;
            19/8/29-23/8/29.
2772/64798 3/11/57-11/9/62c.
2779/64805 31/10/29-4/11/33;
            2/12/33-30/3/47.
2780/64806 15/11/29-20/6/30;
            19/8/30-9/8/43.
2781/64807 19/11/29-9/8/43.
2975/64836 2/3/41-9/8/43.
1927/64955 30/10/43-30/3/47;
            3/11/57-25/11/60.
3089/64979 13/10/41-8/8/43.
3090/64980 13/10/41-30/3/47.

J50

3228/68927 13/10/46-19/10/52;
            23/11/52-5/2/56.
3230/68929 25/8/46-19/10/52.
3236/68935 13/10/46-22/1/50.
2789/68972 13/10/46-29/2/48.
2792/68975 25/8/46-19/10/52;
            23/11/52-14/6/53;
            5/7/53-30/10/55.
2793/68976 25/8/46-19/10/52;
            23/11/52-14/12/58.
606/68982 2/2/39-13/7/47.

J52

4226/68825 19/10/52-23/11/52.
4252/68851 19/10/52-7/12/52.
4284/68883 19/10/52-23/11/52.

J59

6451   *at* 7/23-11/7/25.

J67

7332/68495 11/10/45-18/11/45;
            10/2/46-2/6/46.

J69

7194/68601 2/6/27-16/6/27.

K2

4642/61732 4/1/48-22/2/48.
4664/61754 28/5/25-1/1/27.
4665/61755 28/5/25-7/1/27.

The two K2's which arrived in 1925 spent much of their time at Annesley working the coal and fast goods trains south to Woodford. No.1732 had seven weeks at Annesley in early 1948 but was not sent there for any specific purpose and after a short spell on the main line goods trains to Woodford it returned to Colwick from whence it came.

K3

4001/61801 30/10/43-12/10/47.
4004/61805 6/11/43-17/6/46.
4007/61807 30/11/43-17/6/46.
4008/61808 30/10/43-12/10/47.
58/61820 11/7/31-27/6/33.
73/61822 13/10/40-3/5/43.
80/61824 29/6/47-13/7/47.
109/61827 1/8/31-6/2/34.
120/61834 13/10/40-3/5/43.
121/61835 13/10/40-20/6/43.
140/61841 30/9/39-1/3/40.
159/61848 13/10/31-30/10/35;
            16/7/41-3/5/43.
188/61856 30/1/55-17/5/59.
208/61865 30/9/39-1/3/40.
228/61867 13/10/40-3/5/43.
229/61868 13/10/40-3/7/43.
1300/61870 28/11/40-3/5/43.
2765/61894 30/10/43-6/1/46;
            29/6/47-13/7/47.
2766/61895 30/10/43-21/3/48.

Class K3 cont./

2934/61925 30/10/43-6/1/46.
2438/61943 12/9/48-20/9/53.
2455/61964 17/7/41-3/5/43.
2499/61972 24/10/43-18/11/45.
3814/61974 30/10/43-30/1/55.
3815/61975 30/10/43-16/9/56;
        18/11/56-17/5/59.
3816/61976 30/10/43-27/9/53.
3817/61977 30/10/43-17/2/52.
3819/61979 30/10/43-20/9/53.
3820/61980 30/10/43-17/5/59.
3821/61981 30/10/43-18/11/45.
3822/61982 28/11/40-3/5/43;
        30/10/43-17/6/46.

L1(L3)

5273/69051 8/11/19-10/3/23.
5274/69052 8/11/19-10/3/23.
5337/ E9056 8/11/19-10/3/23.
5340/ 9059 10/3/23-18/2/29.
5343/ 9062 12/3/20-9/2/29.
5345/69064 7/1/20-12/3/29.
5366/69065 2/2/23-23/2/29.
5370/69069 9/4/20-2/11/27;
        14/4/28-23/2/29.

N4

5620/69231 14/2/29-26/2/31.

N5

5523/69257 9/8/53-30/8/53.
5525/69259 6/3/38-13/10/46.
5526/69260 26/7/42-18/8/46.
5748/69286 18/3/32-24/7/42;
        13/6/48-4/12/49.
5758   7/3/32-27/11/37c.
5764/69304 ?/12/17-4/5/33.
5765/69305 8/3/10-8/5/38.
5767/69307 2/11/18-20/9/33.
5770/69310 19/2/01-8/8/24;
        7/11/24-21/2/34;
        26/6/35-14/8/35.
5774   1/1/23-8/8/24;
        7/11/24-21/2/34.

5775/69314 1/1/23-4/2/39.
5051/69315 3/12/32-13/10/46.
5923/69347 8/5/38-18/8/46.
5926/69350 27/3/38-13/10/46.
5927/69351 29/12/22-3/12/32.
5930/69354 2/10/15-19/4/34.
5937/69361 25/9/15-2/12/27.
5939/69363 22/3/13-13/2/29.

N7

873/69651 23/12/51-30/9/56.
2651/69691 4/11/51-30/5/54.
2655/69695 4/11/51-16/5/54.

N15

9910/69147 10/7/24-16/11/24.

O1 (Thompson)

6224/63571 27/8/49-3/3/57.
6231/63578 16/7/50-17/11/62c.
6232/63579 16/1/49-24/2/57;
        14/4/57-21/11/62c.
6242/63589 30/4/49-3/11/57.
6243/63590 26/11/50-3/3/57.
6244/63591 26/11/50-17/11/62c.
6245/63592 26/11/50-3/11/57.
5333/63594 16/1/49-3/11/57.
6249/63596 30/7/49-17/2/57.
5385/63610 23/1/49-21/11/62c.
5394/63619 26/11/50-3/3/57.
6555/63630 26/11/50-3/3/57.
6374/63646 2/7/50-24/2/57.
6545/63650 26/11/50-17/2/57.
6371/63652 26/11/50-10/2/57.
6359/63663 26/11/50-24/2/57.
6356/63670 26/11/50-10/2/57.
6350/63676 2/9/51-21/11/62c.
5408/63678 23/12/44-7/1/45;
        26/11/50-24/2/57.
6324/63687 19/2/48-7/3/48;
        23/4/50-10/2/57.
6341/63689 16/7/50-17/11/62c.
6195/63711 26/11/50-17/11/62c.
6328/63725 26/11/50-15/7/56;
        16/12/56-24/2/57.

6566/63740 2/9/51-17/11/62c.
6571/63746 5/12/48-3/3/57.
6575/63752 20/2/48-7/3/48;
        2/7/50-17/11/62c.
6513/63768 26/11/50-3/11/57.
6213/63773 26/11/50-24/2/57.
6214/63777 20/10/50-26/10/62c.
6505/63780 20/10/50-10/2/57.
6507/63784 26/11/50-26/5/57.
6515/63786 27/10/50-3/3/57.
6216/63789 26/11/50-17/11/62c.
6283/63792 13/2/49-26/10/62c.
6595/63795 2/4/50-17/2/57.
6596/63796 22/10/50-17/2/57;
        14/4/57-26/10/62c.
6220/63803 16/7/50-17/2/57.
6601/63806 23/1/49-21/11/62c.
6519/63808 16/7/50-17/11/62c.
6263/63817 26/11/50-17/11/62c.
6261/63838 19/6/49-26/10/62c.
6526/63854 26/11/50-17/11/62c.
6533/63863 16/7/50-3/11/57.
6535/63865 26/11/50-17/11/62c.
6624/63867 31/1/49-17/11/62c.
6625/63868 2/7/50-17/2/57.
6626/63869 2/7/50-17/11/62c.
6525/63872 26/11/50-26/5/57.
6288/63879 4/11/44-3/12/44;
        23/4/50-10/2/57.
6635/63886 22/10/50-26/10/62c.
6636/63887 26/11/50-14/4/57.
6639/63890 26/11/50-14/4/57.
6642/63901 2/7/50-17/11/62c.

Thirty of the Thompson O1 class were ousted from Annesley during 1957 with the arrival of an equal number of BR 9F's which took over the fast freights to Woodford and more besides. Twenty-five of the thirty went to March in exchange for the 9F's and the other five went to Colwick shed. By the end of 1962, when the depot was under London Midland Region control, the remaining twenty-odd Thompson O1's were condemned virtually en masse; some of them only a few weeks ex-works from general overhauls. The class was replaced at Annesley by the LMS 8F 2-8-0 which although was no more efficient than the former LNER 2-8-0 it was obviously more favoured by the LMR authorities. Because of the boundary changes with the regional shake-up, the O1's went for scrapping to Crewe and Derby works rather than Gorton or perhaps Doncaster - it was certainly a funny period when virtually anything out of the ordinary could and did indeed happen.

O2

3840/63970 20/2/48-7/3/48.
3857/63987 20/2/48-7/3/48.

These 2-8-0's came from Langwith Junction shed and returned there after what was a two week 'loan' for traffic purposes.

O4

6223/63570 ?/10/12-6/6/29.
6224/63571 ?/10/12-20/9/19;
        12/10/47-7/5/49, to O1.
6225   ?/11/12-21/3/35.
6226/63573 ?/11/12-12/2/39;
        18/4/48-26/12/48;
        17/9/50-26/11/50.
6227/63574 ?/11/12-9/3/29.
6228/63575 ?/11/12-23/1/49;
        5/2/50-16/7/50.
6238   17/3/15-19/9/41 to WD.
6239   16/2/24-28/9/39.
5069/63580 12/10/47-6/2/49;
        18/12/49-26/11/50.
5093/63582 12/10/47-22/1/50.
6242/63589 22/1/39-30/5/39;
        12/10/47-20/2/48.
6249/63596 12/10/47-30/4/49, to O1
6252/63599 11/4/48-8/1/50.
5271   2/11/18-2/2/23.
5375   24/7/15-11/10/41 to WD
5377/63602 22/1/56-11/11/56.
5380/63605 23/11/17-5/4/24;
        14/10/27-29/6/47.

Class O4 cont./

5381/63606	11/3/24-5/4/24; 6/9/27-11/8/44.
5382	13/3/24-5/4/24.
5383	27/3/24-31/3/24.
5385	29/3/24-5/4/24.
5387/63612	7/9/17-5/4/24.
5388/63613	30/3/47-29/6/47.
5389/63614	?/9/18-29/6/47; 12/10/47-26/11/50.
5393/63618	2/10/43-8/10/50; 30/9/51-24/2/52.
5394/63619	3/11/27-23/12/44, to O1
6556/63631	12/10/47-1/2/48; 4/12/49-16/7/50.
6536/63633	12/10/47-2/4/50.
5351/63635	18/3/15-29/6/47; 12/10/47-26/11/50.
6376/63636	30/3/47-29/6/47.
6375/63638	12/10/47-8/2/48; 14/11/48-18/12/49.
6559/63639	30/5/48-28/9/52; 22/1/56-17/6/56.
6560	23/2/29-13/9/41 to WD.
6561/63641	23/5/48-16/7/50.
6358/63662	12/10/47-8/2/48; 6/6/48-26/11/50.
6368	10/5/24-15/2/34.
6356/63670	15/5/31-23/5/38.
6354/63672	10/2/34-20/11/38.
6351/63674	18/12/49-28/9/52.
6353/63675	15/5/24-20/11/38.
5408/63678	28/7/21-1/8/44, to O1.
6347/63681	6/1/46-29/6/47; 12/10/47-26/11/50.
6344/63685	26/10/47-9/5/48.
6495/63686	25/1/33-7/5/44; 9/5/48-2/7/50.
6349/63694	21/2/29-29/6/47; 12/10/47-28/3/48; 30/1/49-5/2/50.
6496/63695	26/1/33-7/5/44; 4/7/48-2/7/50.
6323/63696	4/4/24-28/9/39.
6337/63699	12/10/47-8/10/50; 30/9/51-4/11/51.
6339	25/6/30-14/9/41 to WD.

6192/63700	12/10/47-8/2/48; 23/1/49-26/11/50.
6321/63702	21/12/35-25/11/40; 8/10/50-26/11/50.
6320/63705	21/4/24-5/9/43.
6319/63706	12/10/47-20/2/48; 7/3/48-26/11/50.
6553/63713	11/4/48-30/1/49; 5/2/50-2/7/50.
6310/63716	12/10/47-26/11/50.
6311/63720	12/10/47-8/2/48.
6331/63721	23/5/48-19/9/48; 4/12/49-22/10/50.
6199/63722	12/10/47-26/11/50.
6200/63723	12/10/47-8/10/50.
6202	15/2/34-19/9/41 to WD.
6309/63729	15/5/24-25/11/40.
6307/63731	21/4/24-5/9/43.
6562/63735	1/4/45-29/6/47; 12/10/47-11/9/49.
6285/63739	26/10/47-20/10/50.
6568/63742	12/10/47-20/10/50.
6206/63743	12/10/47-20/10/50.
6258/63748	7/5/44-26/11/50.
6278/63750	28/3/48-16/1/49.
6574/63751	18/10/53-27/12/53.
6575/63752	6/10/37-13/10/40.
6255/63756	30/3/47-4/7/48.
6282/63759	12/10/47-23/2/49.
6209/63761	7/5/44-29/6/47; 12/10/47-22/1/50; 8/10/50-26/11/50.
6210/63762	30/3/47-28/3/48; 19/9/48-10/7/49.
6212	15/8/25-10/9/41 to WD.
6274/63767	18/2/29-8/10/50.
6213/63773	16/9/12-30/9/44.
6267/63776	1/4/24-6/10/31.
6214/63777	23/9/12-13/10/40.
6215/63778	23/9/12-4/6/29.
6269/63781	18/4/48-15/5/49; 17/9/50-26/11/50.
6273	6/10/37-11/10/41 to WD
6591/63787	18/12/49-8/1/50; 8/10/50-26/11/50.
6216/63789	25/9/12-20/9/19.
6217	29/9/12-19/9/41 to WD.
6277/63794	12/10/47-16/7/50.

6218/63797	29/9/12-16/2/34; 6/6/48-16/1/49.
6275/63798	6/6/48-28/9/52.
6219/63799	13/11/12-20/10/50.
6598/63801	12/10/47-8/2/48; 14/11/48-11/9/49; 2/9/51-4/11/51.
6599	22/2/37-19/9/41 to WD.
6220/63803	?/11/12-24/11/40.
6512/63804	12/10/47-5/2/50.
6221/63805	?/11/12-19/2/48; 7/3/48-5/12/48; 5/2/50-2/7/50.
6222/63809	12/10/47-20/2/48; 7/3/48-31/1/49.
6264/63818	4/4/24-30/1/25.
6266	18/8/25-23/5/38.
6262/63819	21/4/24-15/5/30.
6306/63827	23/5/48-17/9/50.
6304/63829	12/10/47-1/2/48; 19/9/48-18/12/49; 8/1/50-23/4/50; 8/10/50-26/11/50.
6302/63841	12/10/47-26/11/50.
6614/63845	22/1/56-11/11/56.
6291/63848	23/5/48-23/4/50.
6299/63851	14/3/29-11/8/44; 6/1/46-8/1/48; 26/12/48-8/1/50; 8/10/50-28/9/52.
6292/63853	3/12/44-29/6/47; 12/10/47-26/11/50.
6619/63858	6/2/49-26/11/50.
6620/63859	23/2/29-16/6/49; 17/9/50-26/11/50.
6532/63862	22/2/35-2/7/50.
6629/63873	12/10/47-26/11/50.
6528/63876	30/3/47-20/11/49.
6288/63879	1/10/43-26/8/44, to O1.
6293/63893	12/10/47-8/10/50.
6300/63894	7/1/45-19/9/48; 28/11/48-18/12/49; 2/9/51-31/8/52.
6296/63895	28/3/48-16/7/50.
6640/63899	12/10/47-1/2/48; 6/6/48-5/2/50.
5010/63912	12/10/47-26/11/50.

Where certain O4's went direct from Annesley's allocation for rebuilding to O1 has been noted but, those O4's which were rebuilt to O1 class and did not go to works 'via' Annesley have the notation omitted. The same applies to those O4's which were withdrawn in 1941 for Government service.

After the end of September 1952 very few O4's were to be allocated to Annesley shed, the bulk of the work formely undertaken by this class being entrusted by now to another Gorton product - the Thompson O1.

O7 (WD 2-8-0)

3000/90000	30/3/47-12/10/47.
3001/90001	15/4/51-2/9/51.
3002/90002	30/3/47-12/10/47.
3010/90010	29/6/47-12/10/47.
3014/90014	30/3/47-12/10/47.
3021/90021	1/2/48-11/4/48.
3025/90025	8/2/48-23/5/48; 14/1/51-2/9/51.
3026/90026	29/6/47-12/10/47.
3027/90027	8/2/48-11/4/48.
3036/90036	1/2/48-23/5/48.
3043/90043	6/2/49-8/5/49.
3052/90052	15/4/51-2/9/51.
3068/90068	1/2/48-23/5/48.
3069/90069	29/6/47-11/11/47; 8/2/48-23/5/48.
3073/90073	30/3/47-25/11/47; 8/2/48-20/6/48.
3079/90079	30/3/47-12/10/47.
3100/90100	29/6/47-12/10/47.
3102/90423	29/6/47-12/10/47.
3116/90437	6/2/49-15/5/49.
3127/90448	6/2/49-8/5/49.
3145/90466	29/6/47-1/12/47.
3157/90478	8/2/48-23/5/48.
3163/90484	29/6/47-12/10/47.
3170/90491	29/6/47-12/10/47.
3171/90492	14/1/51-2/9/51.
3178/90499	30/3/47-12/10/47.
3184/90505	8/2/48-23/5/48.
3191/90512	29/6/47-12/10/47.

Class WD cont./
3192/90513 29/6/47-12/10/47.

Very few of the WD Austerity 2-8-0's were allocated to Annesley in the British Railways period. Although there was a sudden influx during the last year of the LNER most of these had gone by Nationalisation. A few examples were 'on the books' between 1948 and 1951 but much of the work they did was being handled by the Thompson O1's as that class grew numerically. According to Annesley men, the WD was something of a rough rider when heading the fast freights to Woodford and back.

Q4

5064/ 3205	5/1/31-28/12/35.
5067/63207	9/1/31-14/4/36.
5963	9/3/29-22/5/31.
6179/(3242)	10/3/24-15/4/36.

SENTINEL 2-CYLINDER RAILCARS

12ᴇ/43306	29/6/31-23/12/32;
	6/7/37-20/4/40c.
13ᴇ/43307	20/9/30-22/1/40c.

SENTINEL 6-CYLINDER RAILCARS

51908	26/1/41-30/10/43c.
51912	11/11/39-4/10/43.
51915	25/5/40-29/11/40;
	6/3/41-4/5/41.

CLAYTON RAILCARS

2122/43303	7/7/29-26/5/30.

The Clayton and Sentinel railcars all took their turn on the Annesley 'Dido' workings and between 1929 and 1943 there was always at least one of the steam railcars available for work.

Ex LMS Locomotives

LMS 4P 2-6-4T

42333	1/59-1/60.
42339	1/59-1/60.
42361	1/59-1/60.

LMS 2-6-0 5MT

42769	1/59-11/61.
42784	1/59-11/61.
42847	1/59-6/60.
42872	1/59-7/60.
42897	1/59-6/60.

LMS Cl.5 4-6-0

44665	5/62-10/65.
44717	9/62-7/65.
44835	10/64-10/65.
44846	3/63-7/65.
44847	7/64-10/65.
44848	7/64-1/66.
44932	1/60-1/63;
	2/63-6/65;
	7/65-12/65.
44984	7/64-1/66.
45116	1/60-1/63.
45190	10/64-3/65;
	8/65-10/65.
45215	6/60-6/65.
45217	6/60-5/63.
45223	1/60-8/61.
45234	1/60-2/63;
	3/63-6/65.
45267	9/62-3/63;
	10/64-3/65;
	7/65-1/66.
45289	10/64-3/65.
45301	7/64-7/65c.
45333	10/64-10/65.
45334	5/63-6/65c.
45335	9/64-7/65c.
45342	7/64-6/65.
45346	7/64-6/65.
45405	10/64-10/65.
45416	7/64-7/65c.
45450	1/60-6/65.

LMS 'Jubilee' 4-6-0

45626	11/62-1/63.
45735	10/63-9/64c.

LMS 'Royal Scot' 4-6-0

46101	1/63-8/63c.
46111	1/63-9/63c.
46112	9/62-5/64c.
46114	9/63-9/63c.
46122	12/62-10/64.
46125	9/63-9/64c.
46126	11/62-9/63c.
46143	9/62-12/63c.
46153	9/62-12/62c.
46156	10/63-10/64c.
46158	9/62-10/63c.
46163	1/63-8/64c.
46165	2/64-11/64.
46167	9/63-4/64c.
46169	1/63-5/63c.

LMS 8F 2-8-0

48002	9/62-2/63.
48005	9/62-12/62.
48007	10/62-2/63.
48011	9/62-8/63.
48024	9/62-5/64;
	5/65-6/65.
48037	5/63-6/65.
48053	5/65-6/65.
48057	9/62-7/65.
48064	9/62-5/64.
48079	9/62-6/65.
48099	9/62-11/63.
48117	9/62-8/64.
48141	9/62-6/65.
48142	9/62-8/65.
48166	5/63-6/65.
48168	9/62-6/65.
48220	9/58-1/59;
	9/62-12/62.
48293	9/62-6/65.
48304	9/62-6/65.
48315	9/58-1/59.
48324	9/62-6/65.
48333	9/62-5/63.
48356	5/65-6/65.
48363	12/64-6/65.
48378	9/62-8/65c.
48615	9/62-5/63.
48661	12/64-6/65.
48678	7/56-12/56;
	4/63-5/64.
48700	9/62-8/64.
48727	5/63-7/63.
48770	9/62-5/63.

BR Standard Locomotives

BR BRITANNIA 4-6-2

70014	6/62-10/62.
70015	6/62-10/62.
70048	6/62-10/62.
70049	6/62-10/62.

The four Britannia's which graced Annesley's yard from June to October 1962 were the depot's first and only Pacific tender engines and had come from Neasden shed. When, after a seemingly short stay, they were reallocated in October, all four returned to the London area but this time to Willesden shed.

BR Standard 2-6-2T

84006	4/62-7/64.
84007	3/62-12/63.
84027	3/62-5/64c.

BR Standard 9F

92009	10/58-11/58.
92010	2/57-3/63.
92011	5/57-8/65.
92012	6/57-8/63.
92013	2/57-9/59;
	10/59-6/65.
92014	2/57-3/60;
	10/61-5/65.
92025	4/64-11/64.
92027	4/64-11/64.
92030	6/57-6/65.
92031	5/57-6/65.
92032	6/57-6/65.
92033	6/57-6/65.
92043	2/57-12/65.
92052	10/61-4/62.
92057	10/61-4/63.
92067	2/57-6/65.
92068	2/57-4/64;
	6/65-12/65.
92069	2/57-5/65.

92070	2/57-3/60.
92071	2/57-7/65.
92072	2/57-6/65.
92073	3/57-6/65.
92074	3/57-6/65.
92075	3/57-4/63;
	10/63-6/65.
92076	3/57-10/63.
92081	11/58-5/59.
92083	11/60-3/61;
	2/63-3/63;
	1/65-5/65.
92087	3/57-6/65.
92088	3/57-5/63;
	8/63-6/65.
92089	3/57-2/63.
92090	3/57-5/65.
92091	3/57-7/65.
92092	3/57-5/65.
92093	3/57-6/65.
92094	4/57-11/58;
	5/59-5/65.
92095	3/57-6/65.
92096	4/57-12/65.
92110	11/63-9/64.
92111	11/63-9/64.
92113	10/64-6/65.
92117	10/61-3/62.
92120	10/58-11/58;
	11/60-10/61.
92129	10/61-12/61.
92132	3/64-6/65.
92154	5/58-9/58;
	2/64-7/65.

The first 9F based at Annesley was 92010, loaned from March shed in 1956 for trials after which it returned to the Cambridgeshire depot. The engine returned to Annesley in February of the following year but this time with nine other 2-10-0's from both Doncaster and March sheds. During the third month of 1957 another eleven 9F's arrived from Doncaster shed and a newly built example (92095) came direct from Swindon works. The second day of April saw another new engine, 92096 also from Swindon, arrive to boost the 9F complement for the time being. During May and June some of the older Eastern Region 9F's were sent to Annesley, and in 1958 the shed had no fewer than thirty of the type allocated - at the time one of the largest concentrations of the BR Standard 2-10-0 in the country. Some good mileages were being put up by the 9F's on the Woodford jobs with 300 or more round trips per annum being recorded for some engines during 1959 and 1960. However, they were capable of nearly twice that number but in the event the amount of traffic needed to fulfill the anticipated utilization of the class was not there and what was, was rapidly ebbing away.

USA S160 2-8-0.

Although never allocated at Annesley, these 2-8-0's which were on loan to the LNER during the war years 1942 to 1945, were regular daily visitors to Annesley shed after working in from Woodford. Annesley men were trained to drive and fire them and indeed did so. The number range of these Woodford based engines was as follows:-

1704, 1706, 1707, 1709, 1710, 1729, 1730, 1731, 1829, 1832, 1833, 1834, 1836, 1839, 1840, 1844, 1846, 1847, 1848, 1849, 2048, 2049, 2050, 2051 2057.

Amongst the more 'exotic' steam engines which regularly visited Annesley were the Great Eastern 0-6-0's (LNER Class J15, J16 and J17) which during pre-Grouping days and indeed throughout the early LNER period, worked in from March (Whitemoor) via the former Lancashire, Derbyshire & East Coast line. Usually three of these 0-6-0's would work in each day with separate trains of coal empties and return with full loads. Engine servicing and turning was carried out at Annesley shed.

As mentioned earlier, exNorth Eastern six-coupled engines were regular visitors throughout the LNER era and in BR times, B16's from York carried on the tradition and became another regular class of engine visiting for servicing at Annesley shed after working in on through goods trains destined for points south and west of Nottingham.

Wartime brought many new and different classes of engine to Annesley yard, amongst those from the North Eastern area were the Q6 0-8-0's which were sometimes pressed into further service south to Woodford.

BR Diesel Locomotives

350 h.p. 0-6-0 DIESEL ELECTRIC.

D3859	7/11/59-?
D3860	14/11/59-?
D3861	21/11/59-?

These are the only diesel locomotives known to have been shedded at Annesley depot, being used in the adjacent yards. All three arrived new from Horwich works in November 1959 when the shed was part of the LMR. When these diesel shunters actually left Annesley is not known but it was probably some months prior to the closure of the depot, if not before. Where they went for 'everyday' maintenance is also unknown but possibly Langwith Jct or Westhouses sheds were the venues as required.